The Craziest Joke Book Ever

This is the ultimate in Crazy Joke
books, crammed with all kinds of
hilarious nonsense to make you fall
about with laughter. There are 'doctor'
jokes, 'knock-knock' jokes, jokes
about teachers and waiters, parents
and children – all guaranteed to keep
you in stitches.

    This is the fourth Crazy Joke book
published by Beaver. The others are
called *The Crazy Joke Book*, *More
Crazy Jokes* and *Even Crazier Jokes*.

THE CRAZIEST JOKE BOOK EVER

Compiled by Janet Rogers

Illustrated by Robert Nixon

Beaver Books

A Beaver Original
Published by Arrow Books Limited
17-21 Conway Street, London W1P 6JD
A division of the Hutchinson Publishing Group
London Melbourne Sydney Auckland Johannesburg
and agencies throughout the world

First published in 1982
Fourth impression 1984
© Copyright text Victorama Limited 1982
© Copyright illustrations
The Hutchinson Publishing Group 1982

Set in Times
Printed and bound in Great Britain by
Anchor Brendon Limited, Tiptree, Essex

ISBN 0 600 20609 2

Introduction

Yes, here it is! At long last Beaver Books proudly presents the joke book that the whole world has been waiting for: *THE CRAZIEST JOKE BOOK EVER!*

We have searched the universe to bring you the craziest jokes imaginable – and some of them really are quite out of this world. . . .

What's small and green and flies a U.F.O.?
An airsick Martian, of course! . . .

Thankfully others are rather more down to earth. . . .

Sign in a cafeteria in Holland: 'Mothers, please wash your Hans before eating.'

In the pages that follow you'll find jokes to cover every possible subject – from hearing-aids. . . .

I've just invented a hearing-aid that doesn't need batteries. It's a sign you hang round your neck that reads: PLEASE SHOUT. . . .

to hospitals. . . .

Doctor, this is the third operating table you've ruined this week. You must learn not to cut so deeply!

You don't *have* to be crazy to read this book, but if you are it certainly helps! Have fun.

J.R.

Two drunks were staggering home one night. One looked up to the sky and said: 'Is that the sun or the moon?'

'I don't know,' replied the other, 'I don't live around this area.'

DOCTOR: *I'm terribly sorry to have to tell you this, Mrs Beasley, but you have rabies.*
MRS BEASLEY: Quick, get me a piece of paper.
DOCTOR: *What for? To write a will?*
MRS BEASLEY: No, to make a list of people I want to bite.

'*I was sorry to hear that the hurricane blew your house away with your wife still inside it.*'
'That's all right. She's been wanting a holiday for a long time.'

Why do elephants drink so much water?
Nobody ever thinks to give them anything else.

A man was in a restaurant. He had one arm in a sling and his empty sleeve was trailing in another man's soup.

'Hey! You've got your sleeve in my soup!' shouted the diner.

The first man replied: 'Don't worry, there's no 'arm in it.'

Knock, knock.
Who's there?
Cook.
Cook who?
Good gracious. It's one o'clock already.

He who laughs last doesn't get the joke.

'Did you hear my last joke?'
'I certainly hope so!'

JOHNNY: *How did you break your arm?*
TOMMY: Do you see those cellar steps?
JOHNNY: *Yes.*
TOMMY: Well, I didn't.

'Doctor, Doctor, there's something wrong with my stomach.'
'Well, keep your coat buttoned up and no one will notice!'

What happened to the man who ate a lot of sugar?
He got a lump in his throat.

Knock, knock.
Who's there?
Sabina.
Sabina who?
Sabina long time since I've seen you.

What did the baby hedgehog say when it backed into a cactus?
Is that you, Mother?

PATIENT: *I feel half dead.*
DOCTOR: I'll make arrangements for you to be buried up to your waist.

ROGER: *Did your watch stop when it hit the floor?*
DODGER: Well it didn't go straight through, silly!

What is a down-to-earth story?
One about a parachute jumper.

Why is it bad to write on an empty stomach?
Because paper is better.

In this world you've got to be crazy or else you would go nuts!

Knock, knock.
Who's there?
Noah.
Noah who?
Noah good place to eat?

Advertisement for a new kind of soap:
'Use Dopey Soap. It doesn't lather, it doesn't bubble, it won't get you clean, but it's tremendous company in the bath.'

A solicitor was reading the will of the late Donald Wopsledown, and had just reached the final paragraph: 'I always said that I would remember my dear wife, Mavis, and mention her in my will. So, hi there, Mave!'

WOODWORK TEACHER: *What are you making, Edgar?*
EDGAR: I'm making a portable.
WOODWORK TEACHER: *A portable what?*
EDGAR: I don't know, I've only made the handles so far.

'*Darling, how could I ever leave you?*'
'By bus, train, tram, plane, taxi, bike. . . .'

Gormless Gavin took Nervous Nigel out driving on a very narrow road.
   'I feel very scared when you go around those sharp bends,' admitted Nigel.
   'You should do what I do,' said Gavin, 'close your eyes.'

Two fat men ran in a race. One ran in short bursts, the other in burst shorts.

'*Can you stand on your head?*'
'No, it's too high.'

BARRY: *My sister's a maniokleptic.*
HARRY: Don't you mean a kleptomaniac?
BARRY: *No, she walks backwards into shops and leaves things.*

'*Have you any blue ties to match my eyes?*'
'No, but we've got some soft hats to match your head.'

Why were two flies playing football in a saucer?
They were practising for the cup.

What is the advantage of being bald?
You can style your hair with a damp cloth!

ANTIQUE DEALER: *This is Oliver Cromwell's skull.*
COLLECTOR: How can it be? It's much too small.
ANTIQUE DEALER: *Yes, well this was his skull when he was a little boy.*

What do you do if you get a button lodged up your nose?
Breathe through those four little holes.

RODDY: *I hear your uncle drowned in a tub of varnish. It must have been awful.*
NOBBY: Yes, but he had a beautiful finish.

10

'I think Grandma needs glasses.'
'Why do you say that, Tony?'
'She's in the kitchen looking at the washing machine.'
'What's wrong with that?'
'She thinks she's watching wrestling on the television.'

If you hear a good joke, don't take it home. That's carrying it a bit too far.

'How do you like my new toupee?'
'It looks great, you can't tell it isn't a wig.'

BASIL: *Who's that at the door?*
BERYL: A man trying to sell a beehive.
BASIL: *Tell him to beehive himself and buzz off.*

What illness do retired pilots get?
'Flu.

'My doctor tells me I can't play golf.'
'So he's played with you too, has he?'

A census-taker knocked on the door of Miss Ruby Briggs. She answered all his questions, but refused to tell him her age.
    'But everybody tells the census-taker their age.'
    'Do you mean Gladys and Doreen Hill at Number 2 told you their age?'
    'Yes.'
    'Well I'm the same age as them,' replied Miss Briggs.
    On his form the census-taker wrote: 'As old as the Hills.'

'Is your mother at home?'
'Well you don't think I'm mowing the lawn because
    I want to, do you?'

11

SAMMY: *One packet of birdseed please.*
PET SHOP OWNER: How many birds have you got?
SAMMY: *None, but I'm going to try and grow some.*

Why do footballers keep so cool?
They have lots of fans.

What did one candle say to the other?
You're getting on my wick.

'*What happened to your Morris car?*'
'Morris took it back.'

Knock, knock.
Who's there?
Pyjamas.
Pyjamas who?
Pyjamas round me, honey, hold me tight. . . .

Why is a kettle like an animal?
Because it is a water otter.

Why do cows lie on sunny beaches?
Because they like tanning their hides.

'I used to be a fortune-teller, but I gave up. There wasn't any future in it.'

What sort of meat do idiots like?
Chump chops.

'*Why did Sheila leave her job?*'
'Due to illness.'
'*Oh, anything serious?*'
'The boss got sick of her.'

12

There was once a man who could not stop singing. He became such a nuisance that eventually he was informed that if he did not stop he would be placed before a firing squad and shot. He still would not stop, so preparations were made for his execution. Just before he was shot he was offered one last request, and he asked if he could sing a final song. His request was granted and he began to sing: 'There were 100 000 green bottles hanging on a wall. . . .'

TEACHER: *If I cut two apples and two bananas into ten pieces each, what will I get?*
SAMMY: A fruit salad.

'Is this train on time?'
'We're satisfied if it's on the track, sir.'

What did the sardines say when they saw a submarine?
There goes a can of people.

DOLLIE: *We were so poor that I was twelve before I realised people ate three meals a day.*
MOLLIE: We were poorer than that. When we were ill we were only allowed one measle at a time.

SILLY: *I had a trip to London yesterday.*
BILLY: Oh, I'm so sorry, did you hurt yourself?

What did one ghost say to the other?
'Do you believe in people?'

DINER: *Waiter, will my hamburger be long?*
WAITER: No, sir, round like everybody else's.

Where does a 250-kg gorilla sleep?
Absolutely anywhere it wants to.

TEACHER: *When was Rome built?*
ROGER: At night.
TEACHER: *What makes you say that?*
ROGER: Well, I heard that Rome wasn't built in a day.

Knock, knock.
Who's there?
Iris.
Iris who?
Iristled for my dog, but he didn't come.

MRS C: *Who's that lady with the little wart?*
MRS D: Keep quiet. That's her husband.

'*Answer the telephone.*'
'But it's not ringing.'
'*Oh, why do you always leave everything until the last minute!*'

Did you hear about the vegetarian cannibal?
He would only eat Swedes.

BOBBY: *Do you have a hobby?*
NOBBY: Yes, I like to sit in a corner and collect dust.

'*You've heard the saying: "A friend in need is a friend indeed"?*'
'Yes, stranger.'

DIDDY: *I know the most amazing sword-swallower. He can swallow a sword two metres long.*
DODDY: What's so strange about that?
DIDDY: *He's only one and a half metres tall.*

GUEST: 'This hotel advertised "bed and board". I don't know which was the bed and which was the board.'

What happened when the hammer was invented?
It made a great impression.

LADY CRABTREE: *And what can I do for you, my man?*
TRAMP: I'd like a coat sewn on this button.

Why was Shakespeare able to write so well?
Because where there's a Will there's a way.

BORIS: *Why do they put telephone wires so high?*
DORIS: To keep up the conversation.

Did you hear about the short-sighted jockey who couldn't find the weigh-in?

BASIL: *My dad's a big-time operator.*
SYBIL: What does he do?
BASIL: *He winds up Big Ben.*

PORTER: *Can I carry your bag, sir?*
MR BROWN: No, let her walk.

There is nothing like bareback horse-riding to make a person feel better off.

ROMULUS: *What's a Grecian urn?*
REMUS: I don't know, I'm too embarrassed to ask.

Why did the owl 'owl?
Because the woodpecker would peck 'er.

What do animals read in zoos?
Gnus papers.

Where would you find the Andes?
At the end of your wristies.

Did you hear about the man who kept banging his head against a brick wall?
Well, you see, he found it was so nice when he stopped.

MRS BROWN: *Did you go to France for your holiday?*
MRS GREEN: I don't know, my husband bought the tickets.

What is sweet, sour and violent?
Take-away kung food.

16

TIMOTHY: *I was once shipwrecked in the ocean and had to live on a tin of baked beans for a week.*
SIDNEY: You were very lucky you didn't fall off.

'My wife has a slight impediment in her speech. Now and again she has to stop and breathe.'

Why did the bus stop?
Because it saw the zebra crossing.

'*Do you like duck?*'
'Duck is my favourite chicken, except for turkey.'

Pamela made her husband a millionaire. Before she married him he was a multi-millionaire.

Did you hear about the snooker-playing thief who pocketed the ball?

BOSS: *I do hope you understand the importance of punctuation?*
NEW SECRETARY: Oh yes, I always get to work on time.

What is the noblest dog of all?
A hot dog, because it feeds the hand that bites it.

LUCY: *I fell over fifty feet this morning.*
LACY: Did you hurt yourself?
LUCY: *No, but I thought I'd never get off the train.*

COOKING TIP: To prevent rice from sticking together, boil each grain separately.

What made the bed spread?
Seeing the pillow slip.

Why are flowers lazy?
They are always found in beds.

'*You want to work here? Can you shoe horses?*'
'No, but I can shoo flies.'

MAN IN SEA: *Help! Help! I can't swim!*
DRUNK ON SHORE: So what? I can't play the piano but I don't boast about it.

What was King Arthur's favourite game?
Knights and crosses.

'*Who told you that you were a good bookkeeper?*'
'The librarian.'

BUTCHER: *Sorry, Sir, we have no ducks today. How about a chicken?*
MAN: Don't be silly. I can't tell my wife I shot a chicken!

MARION: *I do like your hat.*
MARGARET: It's a hunting hat.
MARION: *Why's it called a hunting hat?*
MARGARET: Because my sister will be hunting for it.

What is a string quartet?
Four people playing tennis.

GLORIA: *I'm glad I wasn't born in France.*
MOTHER: Why, Gloria?
GLORIA: *Because I can't speak a word of French.*

Is it true that if you attend a skeleton ball you have a rattling good time?

A man kept reading that cigarettes and sweets were bad for his health. It worried him so much that he gave up reading.

SHERLOCK HOLMES: *Ah, Watson, you are wearing your red thermal underwear.*
DR WATSON: Absolutely amazing, Holmes. How did you deduce that?
SHERLOCK HOLMES: *Elementary, my dear Watson! You've forgotten to put your trousers on again!*

Why is it a waste of time holding a party for chickens?
It's hard to make hens meet.

What made the garden laugh?
The hoe-hoe-hoe.

TEACHER: *I hope I didn't see you looking at someone else's exam paper, Willie.*
WILLIE: I hope so too, Miss.

What do you call a judge with no fingers?
Justice Thumbs.

What do you call a comic play about ghosts?
A phantomime.

MAN: *When I left my last place the landlady cried.*
LANDLADY: Well I shan't. I ask for rent in advance.

'*I've decided to let my hair grow.*'
'How can you stop it?'

MRS C: *I hear you bought some period furniture.*
MRS D: Yes, it went to pieces in a very short period.

If April showers bring May flowers, what do Mayflowers bring?
Pilgrims.

If a man eats dates is he consuming time?

WIFE: *I'm going back to mother!*
HUSBAND: Well, that's better than her coming here.

'*Why did you wake me up? It's still dark.*'
'Well, open your eyes.'

Sign in a health food store:
CLOSED ON ACCOUNT OF SICKNESS.

A teacher walked into her classroom and spotted a girl sitting with her feet in the aisle and chewing gum.
   'Monica,' said the teacher, 'take that gum out of your mouth and put your feet in this instant!'

20

'Did you ever see a cowslip under a bush?'
'No, but I saw a horsefly over the hedge.'

DENTIST: *Open wide, Mrs Case. My goodness! You've got the biggest cavity I've ever seen, the biggest cavity I've ever seen!*
MRS CASE: You don't have to repeat yourself!
DENTIST: *I wasn't. That was an echo.*

DINER: *Could I have a glass of water, please?*
WAITER: To drink?
DINER: *No, I want to rinse out a few things.*

Why did the man wear sunglasses on rainy days?
To protect his eyes from umbrellas.

BEN: *What time is it?*
DEN: I've no idea.
BEN: *I know that, but what time is it?*

'Did you miss me while I was gone?'
'Were you gone?'

What do cannibals eat Chinese people with?
Chap-sticks.

What song did Count Dracula hate?
'Peg O' My Heart.'

What did the surgeon say when he severed an artery?
'Aorta know better.'

ELLEN: *What is your new boyfriend like?*
HELEN: He is mean, low, nasty, ugly, dirty . . . and those are just his good points.

TEACHER: *What is the Order of the Bath, Michael?*
MICHAEL: Mum, Dad, then me.

A woman had just finished inspecting all the suitcases in a shop. When there was only one left she said to the assistant: 'I'm not going to buy anything now, I'm just looking for a friend.'

'Well,' said the assistant wearily, 'why not look in this last one. She might be in there.'

EDNA *(on the telephone)*: *You don't say! No! You don't say!*
EDGAR: Who was that on the phone?
EDNA: *He didn't say.*

Did you hear about the cannibal who liked to stop where they serve lorry drivers?

'Yesterday I was talking to my friend in the telephone booth. But someone wanted to make a call so we had to get out.'

Did you hear about the book called *How to be Happy Without Money*? It costs £12.50.

MRS NOGGIN: *Can you leave me two gallons tomorrow, I want to bathe in milk.*
MILKMAN: Pasteurised?
MRS NOGGIN: *I'll be happy if it comes up to my waist.*

BABY SKUNK: *Can I have a chemistry set for Christmas?*
MOTHER SKUNK: What, and make the house smell!

What yard has four feet?
A back yard with a dog.

What is the best way to prevent diseases caused by biting
insects?
Don't bite any.

Knock, knock.
Who's there?
Beets.
Beets who?
Beets me. I just forgot.

WILLY: *Look at the bunch of cows.*
BILLY: Not bunch, herd.
WILLY: *Heard what?*
BILLY: Of cows.
WILLY: *Of course I've heard of cows.*
BILLY: No, I mean a cow herd.
WILLY: *Well I don't care. I've got no secrets from cows.*

'*Is that you, darling?*'
'Yes – who is calling?'

MAGICIAN: *I can turn this handkerchief into a dove.*
LITTLE BOY: So what? I can walk down the street and
   turn into a shop.

'*Do you think that women talk more than men?*'
'No, they just use more words.'

Did you hear about the man who stayed up all night
trying to work out what happened to the sun when it
went down? It finally dawned on him.

BILBO: *Did you hear what happened to the flea circus?*
BILJO: No, what?
BILBO: *A dog came along and stole the show.*

Who was the trifle's favourite artist?
Bottijelli.

Why does the lion have a fur coat?
He'd look ridiculous in a duffel-coat.

*'Please tell the court why you stabbed your husband
     128 times.'*
'I didn't know how to switch the electric carving knife
     off.'

'How was the new science fiction movie you saw?'
'Oh you know, the same old story – boy meets girl – boy
     loses girl – boy builds new girl.'

Sign on a travel agent's window: PLEASE GO AWAY.

TEACHER: *Louise, will you tell me what a unit of electricity
     is called?*
LOUISE: What?
TEACHER: *Correct.*

Sign in a shop window: EARS PIERCED WHILE YOU WAIT.

JUDGE: *What is the prisoner charged with?*
LAWYER: He is a camera enthusiast, m'lud.
JUDGE: *But you can't put a person in jail because he takes
     lots of photographs.*
LAWYER: He doesn't take photographs, just cameras.

What did one coffee pot say to the other?
Perk up and don't drip.

Why did the robot act silly?
Because he had a screw loose.

Did you hear about the witch who had identical twins?
You couldn't tell which from which.

SIMON: *I had an argument with my girl-friend last night.*
I wanted to go to the circus and she wanted to go to
the ballet.
GRAHAM: Oh, and what was the ballet like?

What's a noisy soccer fan called?
A foot-bawler.

CHEMISTRY TEACHER: *Can anyone tell me the name of a*
deadly poison?
ADAM: Yes, aviation.
CHEMISTRY TEACHER: *Aviation?*
ADAM: That's right. One drop and you're dead.

'Ever since he was eight years old we've been pleading
with our son to run away from home.'

How do you get close to something that has a lot of
money?
Go and lean on the wall of a bank.

NEW EMPLOYEE: *What time do we start work here?*
SECRETARY: Oh, about two hours after we arrive.

MR JONES: *And what do you do for a living?*
MR BONES: *I write.*
MR JONES: *What a coincidence! I read.*

Why are storytellers weird creatures?
Because tales come out of their heads.

Why did the girl keep her violin in a deep-freeze?
Because she liked to play it cool.

NUTTY NIGEL: *What are you making?*
GORMLESS GAVIN: A wonderful new invention.
NUTTY NIGEL: *Ha, ha, ha, ha, ha!*
GORMLESS GAVIN: Go on and laugh. They laughed at
    Edison, they laughed at Baird, they laughed at
    Gobbit.
NUTTY NIGEL: *Who was Gobbit?*
GORMLESS GAVIN: Have you never heard of Augustus
    Gobbit?
NUTTY NIGEL: *No, what did he invent?*
GORMLESS GAVIN: Nothing, but they all laughed at him.

'I'm learning ancient history.'
'So am I. Let's go for a walk and talk about old times.'

26

DOPEY DORA: *We bumped into some old friends yesterday.*
CHEEKY CHARLIE: Oh, your mum was driving again was she?

ARTHUR: *Where do you swim?*
MARTHA: In the spring.
ARTHUR: *I asked you where, not when.*

What do porcupines eat with their cheese?
Prickled onions.

What is green, hairy and takes aspirins?
A gooseberry with a headache.

How do you make an apple puff?
Chase it around the garden.

TEACHER: *What can you tell me about Margaret of Anjou?*
TOMMY: She was very fat, sir.
TEACHER: *What makes you say that? It's new to me.*
TOMMY: Well, sir, it says in my history book 'amongst Henry's stoutest supporters was Margaret of Anjou'.

If milk comes from a cow, where does wine come from?
A wine-ocerous.

MR MUFFIN: *What is your hobby?*
MR NUFFIN: I race pigeons.
MR MUFFIN: *Oh, do you ever beat them?*

'*How do you like your new watch?*'
'It's marvellous! If I wind it fully it does an hour in fifty-five minutes.'

JUDGE: *I don't see why you broke into the same shop three nights in a row.*
PRISONER: Well, your honour, I chose a dress for my wife and had to change it twice.

WIFE: *Look, we've nearly run out of money!*
BURGLAR: All right, wait until the banks are closed and I'll go and get some.

Sign on road: CROSS ROAD HERE.
To which someone had added: TRY AND CHEER IT UP.

WIFE: *I don't know why you complain about my mother, she only comes to visit us twice a year.*
HUSBAND: Yes, but does she have to stay six months every time she comes?

28

RON: *Why did your brother give up his job in the biscuit factory?*
DON: He went crackers.

'Can you lend me five pounds for a week, old dear?'
'Yes, who's the weak old dear?'

MRS NEW: *Darling, today we've been married exactly twelve months.*
MR NEW: It seems more like a year to me.

'Mummy, Mummy, why is Daddy running so fast?'
'Shut up and reload your gun.'

Did you hear about the little girl who went to the corner to see the traffic jam?
A lorry came along and gave her a jar.

Knock, knock.
Who's there?
Anna.
Anna who?
Annanother thing . . . how long do I have to keep knocking on this door?

'What question can never be answered by yes?'
'Are you asleep?'

'Will you still love me when I'm old and fat and ugly?'
'I do, don't I?'

'Will I lose my looks as I get older?'
'I certainly hope so.'

29

A very spoilt child was annoying other passengers by lying in the aisle of the plane. One particularly irritated man turned to the child and said: 'Hey, kid, why don't you go and play outside?'

When the cow slipped and fell on the ice little Avril couldn't stop laughing. She knew there was no point in crying over spilt milk.

MRS A: *Why do they call your son Wonder Boy?*
MRS B: Because people look at him and wonder.

Which famous chiropodist ruled England?
William the Corn Curer.

Knock, knock.
Who's there?
Ina Claire.
Ina Claire who?
Ina Claire day, you can see forever. . . .

Psychiatrists tell us that one out of every five people is mentally ill. So check your friends – if four of them are all right, then it's you!

'Does your husband have a life insurance?'
'No, only fire insurance. He knows where he's going.'

A man woke up in a hospital in Melbourne, Australia, and saw doctors standing around his bed.
    'Have I been brought here to die?' he asked.
    'No,' answered one of the doctors, 'you were brought here yester-die.'

'I would like a dog licence please.'
'Certainly, Madam, what name?'
'Tiddles.'

A cabbage, a tap and a tomato had a race. How did it go?
The cabbage was ahead, the tap was running, and the
tomato tried to ketchup.

What did Hamlet say when he found he was putting on
weight?
'Tubby or not Tubby . . . that is the question!'

'Remember there was a terrible storm like this the night
you asked me to marry you.'
'Yes, it was a dreadful night.'

31

MR JONES: *I hear your son is a writer. Does he write for money?*
MR SMITH: Yes, in every letter we get.

'*I wish you wouldn't whistle while you work.*'
'But Boss, who's working?'

Why is a monkey like a flower?
Because it's a chimp-pansy.

Confucius he say:
An apple a day keeps the doctor away – if aimed correctly.

'*I finally stopped my son biting his nails.*'
'How did you manage that?'
'*I bought him some shoes.*'

JOHNNY: *I don't think I deserve a zero in my exam.*
TEACHER: I quite agree, but I couldn't give you any lower.

MR MORRIS: *I haven't seen you for ages, are you still working for the same people?*
MR AUSTIN: Yes . . . the wife and kids.

Knock, knock.
Who's there?
Huron.
Huron who?
Huron time for once in your life.

I am something that no man wants, but no man wants to lose. What am I?
A bald head.

What has twelve legs, six ears and one eye?
Three blind mice and half a kipper.

When is the cheapest time to ring your friends on the telephone?
When they're out.

PATIENT: *Thank you, Doctor, I feel like my old self again.*
DOCTOR: In that case you need more treatment.

Where does a ghost train stop?
At a manifest-ation.

Do you know why Harry always goes about with his mouth open?
Because he is so lazy, it saves him having to open it when he wants to yawn.

FARMER: *This machine does the work of twenty men. It almost has a brain.*
COWHAND: Not if it does all that work it hasn't!

Knock, knock.
Who's there?
Cargo.
Cargo who?
Cargo Toot! Toot!

TEACHER: *What is water, Clive?*
CLIVE: It's a colourless liquid that turns black when I put my hands in it.

OVERWEIGHT CUSTOMER: *What would you recommend, waiter?*
WAITER: A course of slimming pills, Sir.

What is the difference between a good-natured dog and a bad scholar?
One rarely bites, the other barely writes.

Did you hear about the conceited actor who went to the window and took a bow every time there was a thunderclap?

MR BROWN: *Will you be using your lawn mower all afternoon?*
MR GREEN: Yes, I will.
MR BROWN: *Good, you won't mind me borrowing your car then.*

DOD: *Is that perfume I smell?*
POP: It is – and you do!

LIZA: *Whenever you sing it reminds me of a pirate.*
MINA: Oh, why is that?
LIZA: *Because it's an example of murder on the high Cs!*

Who were the first people to write with fountain pens?
The Incas (inkers).

How long does it take a candle to burn?
About one wick.

Who was the father of the Black Prince?
Old King Cole.

ALBERT: *Where do all the fleas go in winter?*
ALFRED: Search me.

NEWSFLASH: Yesterday a man was drowned in a cesspool. The coroner gave a verdict of sewercide (suicide).

A taxi driver discovered a bag full of kippers had been left in the back of his cab. He took them to the police station and was told that if nobody claimed them within six months they were his.

FATHER: *Do you like moving pictures?*
JIMMY: I certainly do, Dad.
FATHER: *Good, you can help me carry some down from the attic.*

Gestapo officer to prisoners-of-war: 'Today we have a cross-country run. The first back and the last back will be shot. Right, off you go, you two.'

CUSTOMER: *Do you have pigs' feet?*
BUTCHER: Yes, I do.
CUSTOMER: *Well, if you wear shoes nobody will notice.*

Three lunatics were working on a building site, supposedly digging a trench. After a few hours the foreman came along and was surprised to find one of the men digging furiously while the other two were standing motionless, their shovels in the air.

'What are you two doing?' he enquired.

'We're lamp posts,' explained the two lunatics.

The foreman fired the two men immediately and told them to go. But the man in the trench also stopped work.

'It's all right,' said the foreman. 'I haven't fired you. You were working very well, so carry on.'

'I can't,' cried the man. 'How do you expect me to work in the dark?'

'*I gotta "A" in spelling.*'
'You dope! There isn't an "A" in spelling.'

PATIENT: *Doctor, I keep wanting to paint myself all over with gold paint.*

DOCTOR: Oh, that's only your guilt complex.

PATIENT: *It's my mother's fault. She thinks she's a cat.*

DOCTOR: How long has she thought that?

PATIENT: *Ever since she was a kitten.*

'*Do you always snore?*'

'Only when I'm asleep.'

DAVID: *What's your new perfume called?*

JAN: 'High Heaven'.

DAVID: *It certainly smells to it.*

'*Do you think I'm a fool?*'

'No. But what's my opinion against thousands of others?'

Definition of a monologue: a conversation between a woman who has just had an operation and one who hasn't.

DINER: *Waiter, this soup tastes watery.*

WAITER: Just wait until you taste the coffee then.

How do you get your name in the papers?
Walk across a busy street reading one.

What was Camelot famous for?
Its knight life.

What did the Irishwoman sing when her husband started smoking?
'Oh Danny boy, your pipe – your pipe's appalling.'

36

Frank and Sam were climbing a mountain when suddenly Frank slipped and fell down a crevasse 200 metres deep.

He was still alive so his friend lowered down a rope.

'I can't grab it,' shouted Frank, 'my arms are broken.'

'Well, put the rope in your mouth,' shouted Sam.

So Frank put the rope in his mouth and Sam began to pull him to safety – 190 metres . . . 180 metres . . . 175 metres . . . 150 metres . . . 50 metres . . . 25 metres . . . then Sam called out: 'Are you all right, Frank?'

'Yeh-h-h . . . h . . . h. . . .'

DIKKI: *Do you know, for a whole year I couldn't walk?*
NIKKI: How awful! Why was that?
DIKKI: *I wasn't old enough.*

'*Vanessa has just got engaged to an X-ray technician.*'
'I wonder what he sees in her?'

WIFE: *I've given you the best years of my life!*
HUSBAND: So, what do you want? A receipt?

MRS CAMPBELL: *How much are chickens?*
BUTCHER: 80p a pound.
MRS CAMPBELL: *Did you raise them yourself?*
BUTCHER: Yes, this morning they were 70p a pound.

What kind of clothing could you make from tea bags?
A baggy T-shirt.

'*Doctor, what can I do about my broken leg?*'
'Limp.'

'*While you were in Paris did you see the Venus de Milo?*'
'See her! I shook hands with her!'

37

A butcher placed his last chicken on the scales.

'That'll be £3.50,' he said.

'That's much too small, haven't you anything bigger?' asked the customer.

The wily butcher took the chicken back to his fridge, plumped it up a bit, and then brought out the same chicken again.

'This one's £4.50,' he said.

'That's fine,' said the customer, 'I'll take both of them.'

MRS WOOD: *My husband bites his nails.*
MRS NOTT: Well, so do lots of people.
MRS WOOD: *Not six-inch ones! He's a carpenter.*

How do you tell the time by candles?
By the candles-tick.

ETHEL: *My father always gives me a book for my birthday.*
WILF: You must have a fabulous library.

SUSAN: *Dad can't work because Mum broke a leg.*
SADIE: Why can't *he* work if *she* broke the leg?
SUSAN: *Because it was his leg she broke.*

The diner at a restaurant asked the waitress what flavours of ice cream were available.

The waitress answered in a hoarse whisper, 'Vanilla, chocolate and strawberry.'

Wishing to be sympathetic the diner asked, 'Have you got laryngitis?'

'No,' croaked the waitress, 'just vanilla, chocolate and strawberry.'

What did one caterpillar say to the other caterpillar when they saw a butterfly?
'You know, you'd never get me up in one of those things.'

Why did the policeman wear purple braces?
To keep his trousers up.

Why did the man call his dog Johann Sebastian?
Because of his Bach.

'May I hold your hand?'
'No thanks, it isn't heavy.'

What can fly under water?
A fly in a submarine.

39

OLD LADY: *Good heavens! Why are you paddling in your socks?*

LITTLE BOY: Because the water's cold this time of year.

EXAMINER: *It seems to me that you know very little, if anything, about the Bible. Is there any passage you can repeat?*

STUDENT: 'Judas departed and went and hanged himself.'

EXAMINER: *Very good. Perhaps you will repeat another.*

STUDENT: 'Go thou and do likewise.'

A farmer was erecting a building just outside a village, when a visitor stopped to ask him what he was building.

'Well,' replied the farmer, 'if I can let it, it's a rustic cottage. If I can't, it's a cow shed.'

Private Langdon wore a size thirteen in boots. When the sergeant held a roll call all the men were there except for Private Langdon who was nowhere to be seen.

'Anyone here know where Langdon is?' bellowed the sergeant.

'Yes,' said a voice, 'he's gone up to the crossroads to turn round.'

What do you have to do to join Dracula's fan club?
Send your name, address and blood group.

Did you hear about the golfer who cheated so much that when he got a hole-in-one he put a zero on his score card?

'There's a lot of juice in this grapefruit.'
'Yes, far more than meets the eye.'

'I used to wear a flower in my lapel, but I had to give it up.'
'Oh, why?'
'Well, the pot kept hitting me in the stomach.'

A tourist in Switzerland was very alarmed at the steep drop over the side of a mountain, and remarked to the guide, 'This looks very dangerous. You ought to put up a warning sign.'

'Oh,' said the guide, 'we had a warning sign up for two years, but nobody fell over so we took it down again.'

Why is the sky cleaner in New York than in London?
Because there are more skyscrapers.

*Why did the cannibal feel sick each time he ate a
    missionary?*
Because you can't keep a good man down.

Knock, knock.
Who's there?
Sacha.
Sacha who?
Sacha fuss, just because I knocked on the door.

NIKKI: *The dentist wasn't painless like you said he would be.*
FATHER: Why? Did he hurt you?
NIKKI: *No, but he screamed when I bit his finger.*

'*What is the use of reindeer?*'
'It makes the flowers grow, darling.'

When does a cold germ know it has won?
When it brings a man to his sneeze!

KAREN: *Mummy, Mummy, I feel as sick as a dog.*
MOTHER: Don't worry, dear, I'll call a vet.

What do well-behaved lambs say to their mothers?
'Thank ewe!'

SITUATION VACANT: Nanny required for baby with good references.

What is the simplest and quickest way to increase the size of your bank balance?
Look at it through a magnifying glass.

Knock, knock.
Who's there?
Maybelle.
Maybelle who?
Maybelle doesn't ring either.

42

'Do fish grow fast?'
'They certainly do. Every time my dad talks about one
that got away it grows another foot.'

NOKO: *It was so cold last winter our candles froze and we
couldn't blow them out.*
TIPI: It was colder where we live. Our words came out
frozen and had to be put over a fire to find out what we
were saying!

A jigsaw manufacturer in Ireland made his fortune by
inventing the one-piece jigsaw puzzle.

There were two butchers shops side by side in the high
street. Outside one was a sign saying: WE MAKE SAUSAGES
FOR THE QUEEN.
   Outside the shop next door was a sign saying: GOD
SAVE THE QUEEN.

DINER: *What's this insect in my soup?*
WAITER: I wish you wouldn't ask me, I don't know
one bug from another.

Did you hear about the two potatoes who didn't see eye
to eye?

MR PAIN: *Doctor, can you give me something for wind?*
DOCTOR: Yes, here's a kite.

'Well, Doctor, how do I stand?'
'I don't know. It's a miracle.'

DINER: *Waiter, what does this fly in the bottom of my
teacup mean?*
WAITER: How should I know? If you want your fortune
told, go and see a fortune-teller.

WIFE: *They can't do my operation yet, there aren't any beds available.*
HUSBAND: You'll just have to go on talking about the old one for a little longer.

'*Do you like going to the opera?*'
'Apart from the singing, yes.'

FRED: *I was sorry to hear that your mother-in-law died. What was the complaint?*
TED: I haven't heard any yet.

FIRST HUNTER: *Look, here are some lion tracks.*
SECOND HUNTER: Fine. You see where they go and I'll look and see where they come from.

Why did the motorist drive his car in reverse?
Because he knew his Highway Code backwards.

Which dance represents two containers?
The can-can.

A drunk raced after a fire-engine, but collapsed exhausted after a hundred metres. 'All right,' he shouted, 'keep your rotten ice cream!'

What song does the most conceited man in the world sing?
The best things in life are me.

PATIENT: *Doctor, I have a sharp pain in my right foot, what should I do?*
DOCTOR: Walk on the left one.

44

A father was anxious that his young son should grow out of the habit of gambling which he had developed, and asked the help of the boy's headmaster.

When the father called for the boy at the end of term the headmaster said, 'I think I've cured your son of gambling. I'll tell you what happened. One day I saw that he was looking at my beard and he said: "Sir, is that a real beard or a false one? I wouldn't mind betting £5 that it is false." "All right," I replied, "I'll take your bet. Now pull it and see." Of course I made the lad pay £5 so I think I've cured him all right.'

'Oh dear,' groaned the father, 'he bet me £10 that he would pull your beard before the term ended.'

FARMER: *What are you doing in my tree?*
SAMMY: Your sign says 'keep off the grass'.

45

'My brother's teeth are so rotten that every time he sticks his tongue out, one breaks off.'

MOTHER: *Vernon's teacher says he ought to have an encyclopaedia.*
FATHER: Let him walk to school like I had to.

'I've made the chicken soup.'
'Good. I thought it was for us.'

'My wife and I were happy for twenty years. Then we met.'

'Tough luck,' said the egg in the monastery, 'out of the frying-pan into the friar.'

Why did the frankfurter turn red?
It saw the salad dressing.

Knock, knock.
Who's there?
Elke.
Elke who?
Elke seltzer . . . plop, plop, fizz.

What do you do with a wombat?
Play wom of course!

Where would you find a cockney with pimples?
'Ackney.

A man and woman were looking over a house. The estate agent told them, 'It's only a stone's throw from the bus stop.'

46

'OK,' said the man, 'we'll take it. There'll always be something to do in the evening. Throwing stones at buses.'

What do you call two turnips who fall in love?
Swedehearts.

'I like your dress, but isn't it a little early for Hallowe'en?'

PAMELA: *I've played the piano for thirty years – on and off.*
PAUL: Slippery stool?

'Was it crowded at the restaurant last night?'
'Not under my table.'

WAITER: *Would you like your coffee black?*
DINER: What other colours do you have?

Wanted – Person to work on Fissionable Isotope Molecular Atomic Reactive Counters and Triple Phase Cyclotronic Plutonium Hydronamics. *No experience necessary.*

'A funny thing happened to my mother in Birmingham.'
'I always thought you were born in Manchester.'

What makes people shy?
Coconuts.

DINER: *Waiter, there's a fly in my soup.*
WAITER: Sorry, sir, I didn't realise you wished to dine alone.

One day a man happened to be driving past a farm in his car and saw a very beautiful horse. Longing to purchase the animal, he went to the farmer and said: 'I think your horse looks very good and I'll offer you £500 for her.'

'She doesn't look so good, and she's not for sale,' the farmer said.

'I think she looks just fine,' insisted the man, 'and I'll give you £1000 for her.'

'She doesn't look so good,' the farmer replied, 'but if you want her that much, she's yours.'

The man gave the farmer the money and collected the horse. He returned to the farm the next day, however, in a raging temper. Going up to the farmer, he screamed, 'You cheat! You thief! You sold me a *blind* horse!'

Calmly the farmer replied, 'I told you she didn't look so good, didn't I?'

When is it time to get your shoes resoled?
When you tread on a penny and can tell whether it's
    heads or tails.

MOTHER: *How did my little Nigel get a minus one in his exam paper?*
HEADMASTER: Well, he not only got all the questions wrong, but he spelt his name wrong as well.

'Is it raining outside?'
'It doesn't often rain inside.'

DINER: *Waiter, I have a complaint.*
WAITER: This is a restaurant, not a hospital.

What is yellow and goes 'Clunch, clunch'?
A Chinaman eating potato crisps.

48

'Say, mister, your car is smoking!'
'Well, it's old enough.'

Did you hear about a new dance called the 'Lift'?
It has no steps.

VOICE (on telephone): Excuse me, does the night train to
    Edinburgh have a sleeping car?
INFORMATION OFFICER: Yes, it does, sir.
VOICE: Well, wake it up then!

'Doctor, every day when I get home from work my wife
    throws dishes at me, refuses to cook me a meal, and
    calls me awful names.'
'Well that's an easy case. I think perhaps she doesn't
    like you.'

49

FIRST COMIC: *What's your name?*
SECOND COMIC: Hmmmmm . . . let me see . . . 'Happy
  birthday to you, happy birthday to you, happy
  birthday dear Stevie. . . .' It's Stevie.

*'Fancy meeting you here at the psychiatrist's office. Are
  you coming or going?'*
'I don't know. That's why I'm here.'

Heard on a plane 10 000 metres above the Atlantic:
'Ladies and gentlemen. This is your Captain. I have some
good news and some bad news for you. The good news is
that we have perfect visibility, clear weather, and we are
making record time. The bad news is: we are lost!'

'I was so poor as a child that when I was given alphabet
soup it only had one letter in it.'

WOMAN IN CROWD AT THE SALES: *Say! Just who do you
  think you're pushing?*
SECOND WOMAN: I don't know. What's your name?

What does a lamb become after it is one year old?
Two years old.

TEACHER: *Can you tell me the difference between a buffalo
  and a bison?*
COCKNEY CHARLEY: You can't wash your hands in a
  buffalo, Miss.

'Do you play the piano by ear?'
'No, I play it over there.'

MR J: *Why does your wife wear make-up, but no lipstick?*

MR K: She can't keep her mouth still long enough to put it on.

How can you get eggs without keeping hens?
Keep ducks instead.

Why are tall people always the laziest?
Because they are longer in bed than short people.

Knock, knock.
Who's there?
Thistle.
Thistle who?
I suppose thistle have to do.

FIRST MONSTER: *Would you like to play a game of vampires?*
SECOND MONSTER: How do you play that?
FIRST MONSTER: *Oh, for very high stakes.*

Here is the oldest joke in the world:
ADAM: *Do you love me?*
EVE: Who else?

FIRST ROMAN: *What's the time?*
SECOND ROMAN: Half past XII.

What do you get if you cross a cocoa bean with an elk?
A chocolate moose.

Did you hear about the hat designer who decorated his new hats with live birds?
If you don't pay the bill, the hat flies back to the shop.

'*But why did you buy me such a small diamond?*'
'I didn't want the glare to hurt your eyes.'

'*I think golf is a rich man's game.*'
'Rubbish! Look at all the poor players.'

What is green, curly and shy?
Lettuce alone.

Who is very rude and hosts a TV quiz show?
Knickerless Parsons.

Why is the letter F like a cow's tail?
Because it is always on the end of beef.

I was sitting on a train the other day when a gentleman in a fur hat asked the lady next to him: 'D-d-d-d-does th-th-th-this t-t-t-t-t-t-train st-t-t-t-stop at B-B-Bab-Bab-Babbacombe?'

Without answering the lady got up and sat beside me. 'Why didn't you answer his question?' I asked her.

'B-b-b-b-eeeeee-because I d-d-d-didn't w-w-want him t-t-t-to m-m-m-m-m-make f-f-fun of m-m-me,' she replied.

VIOLET: *That salmon in the fishmongers looks nice.*
CISSIE: That's not salmon, it's cod blushing at the price they're asking for it.

HEADMASTER: *Miss Peabody, I am very proud of your teaching and the work your class has produced. How do you manage to keep on your toes with such lively children?*
TEACHER: They put drawing-pins on my chair.

What happened to the bricklayer who fell into the cement mixer?
He became a very hard man.

FREDDY: *Mum, can I have 25p for the man who is crying outside?*
MOTHER: Of course you can, dear. What's he crying about?
FREDDY: *He's crying 'Ice creams 25p! Ice creams 25p!'*

CECIL: *My new girlfriend has beautiful auburn hair all down her back.*
EVELYN: Pity it isn't on her head.

Knock, knock.
Who's there?
Eileen.
Eileen who?
Eileen'd over the fence too far and it broke.

'*Doctor, Doctor, I keep thinking I'm a bird.*'
'Perch there and I'll tweet you in a minute.'

FATHER: *What do you call this?*
JAPONICA: It's cottage pie. I made it at school.
FATHER: *Well, I think I've got a brick in my mouth.*

'*What are you doing in my apple tree, young man?*'
'One of your apples fell down and I'm putting it back.'

54

What was the turtle doing on the M4?
About one mile an hour.

PEDESTRIAN *(lying in the road): What's the matter with you, are you blind?*
DRIVER: Blind! What do you mean blind, I hit you, didn't I?

WAITER: *How did you find your steak, sir?*
DINER: With a magnifying glass.

'My mother had a nervous breakdown trying to fit round tomatoes into square pieces of bread.'

'My, the flies are thick around here.'
'Oh, do you like them thin then?'

ANGRY FISHERMAN: *You've been sitting there for three and a half hours watching me fish! Why don't you try and catch some yourself?*
BYSTANDER: I haven't got the patience.

ENGLISH TEACHER: *'He was bent on seeing her.' Can you put that sentence another way?*
FRANKIE: 'The sight of her doubled him up.'
ENGLISH TEACHER: *Not quite. Try this one. 'Her beauty was timeless.'*
FRANKIE: 'Her face could stop a clock.'

'How did you come to fall in the water?'
'I didn't come to fall in the water. I came to fish.'

MORTON: *Excuse me, I think you're sitting in my seat.*
NUFFIELD: Can you prove it?
MORTON: *I think so. You see I left a treacle tart on it. . . .*

'*What use is your farm? It's six kilometres long, but only five centimetres wide.*'
'I'm going to grow spaghetti.'

OPTICIAN: *Here are your new glasses, but only wear them while you are working.*
PATIENT: That could be difficult.
OPTICIAN: *Why?*
PATIENT: I'm a boxer.

FIRST OCTOPUS: *I don't know what to buy my wife for Christmas.*
SECOND OCTOPUS: Do what I did. Get her four pairs of gloves.

What did the lumberjack do just before Christmas?
He went on a chopping spree.

WIFE (with camera): Well, don't just stand there, get into focus.

What is green, round and smells?
Kermit's bottom.

TEACHER: *Can you give me a sentence that contains the word 'judicious'?*
DELIA: Yes. 'Hands that judicious can be soft as your face.'

'*I understand that your wife came from a fine old family?*'
'Came! She brought them with her!'

WIFE: *Mr MacTavish has invited us for a drink.*
HUSBAND: I wonder which one of us will get it?

GWENDOLINE: *Mum, is it true that we are descended from apes?*

MOTHER: I don't know. I never met your father's family.

'One more word from you and I go back to mother!'
'Taxi!'

'My sister is so modest, she blindfolds herself when she takes a bath.'

HOUSE FLY (to bluebottle): 'I must fly, but I'll give you a buzz later.'

FIRST GHOST: *I don't know about you, but people don't seem to be frightened of me any more.*

SECOND GHOST: No, we might just as well be dead for all they care.

What is black and white and red all over?
An embarrassed zebra!

Why did the ant elope?
Nobody gnu.

SCIENTIST: *I've just crossed a hyena with a tiger.*
ASSISTANT: What did you get?
SCIENTIST: *I don't know, but when it laughs you'd better join in.*

Why did the Romans build straight roads?
So that the Britons couldn't hide round corners.

'Waiter, there's a dead fly in my wine.'
'Well you did ask for something with a little body in it.'

57

'*Doctor, have you got something for my kidneys?*'
'Here's some bacon.'

What did the cannibal say to the famous missionary?
'Dr Livingstone, I consume.'

The booby prize at a nudist camp whist drive was a clothes brush.

PAUL: *Do you know who was on the telly?*
JAMES: Yes, the dog. He isn't trained yet.

How do chickens communicate?
By using fowl language.

BRENDA: *My brother's got a memory like an elephant.*
BREWSTER: Pity he's got a shape to match.

LADY CRABTREE: *What's your name, my man?*
CHAUFFEUR: Charles, madam.
LADY CRABTREE: *I always call my chauffeurs by their surname. What is it?*
CHAUFFEUR: Darling, madam.
LADY CRABTREE: *Drive on, Charles.*

Knock, knock.
Who's there?
Wood.
Wood who?
Wood you believe I've forgotten?

MR BROWN: *I'm afraid my wife has a very biased outlook.*
MR GREEN: Why do you say that?
MR BROWN: *Well, every time we go shopping it's a case of bias this, bias that. . . .*

'What did Sherlock Holmes say to Dr Watson in 1907?'
'I haven't a clue.'

FIRST MAN: *What's the best thing you've seen on television this year?*
SECOND MAN: The 'off' switch.

How much did the psychiatrist charge the elephant?
£15 for the appointment and £150 for the couch.

DOLLY: *There's a man at the door collecting for a new swimming pool.*
MOLLY: Give him a bucket of water.

What did the policeman say to the naughty frog?
'Go on, hop it.'

A woman hired two workmen to put down a new carpet in her lounge. When they had finished they noticed a small bump in the middle of the carpet.

'It must be my packet of cigarettes,' said one man. 'Well, we're not going to take the carpet up again so I'll flatten it.'

He went over and jumped up and down on the lump and flattened the carpet out. At that moment the lady came into the room.

'I've brought you a cup of tea,' she said. 'I found your cigarettes in the kitchen, but there's just one problem. I can't find my pet hamster anywhere. . . .'

'I've boiled this egg for fifteen minutes and it still isn't soft.'

MOTHER: *Harold! Did you fall over in your new trousers?*
HAROLD: Yes, Mum. There wasn't time to take them off.

'Je t'adore,' *he whispered passionately in her ear.*
'Shut it yourself,' she shouted to him.

BILLY: *Mum, can I have another glass of water?*
MOTHER: Another! You've had ten already!
BILLY: *I know, but my bedroom's on fire.*

'*I see much more of Beryl than I used to.*'
'Yes, she has put on a lot of weight recently.'

Does a giraffe get a sore throat if he gets his feet wet?
Yes, but not until two weeks later.

60

FIRST HIPPOPOTAMUS: *What is that creature over there?*
SECOND HIPPOPOTAMUS: It's a rhinoceros.
FIRST HIPPOPOTAMUS: *Fancy having to live with an ugly face like that.*

PASSENGER IN PLANE: *Look at all those people down there. They look just like ants.*
HER HUSBAND: They are ants, you fool – we haven't taken off yet.

'*I'll give a five-pound note to any person who is contented.*'
'I'm quite contented.'
'*If you're quite contented what do you want with five pounds?*'

Why did Henry VIII have so many wives?
Because he liked to chop and change.

How do you make anti-freeze?
Hide her nightie.

'*You remind me of a man.*'
  'What man?'
'*The man with the power.*'
  'What power?'
'*The power of "oo-do".*'
  'Who do?'
'*You do.*'
  'I do what?'
'*Remind me of a man.*'
  'What man?'
'*The man with the power. . . .*'

A man went swimming and while he was gone all his clothes were stolen. What did he come home in?
The dark.

TEACHER: *Have you read* Freckles?
THOMAS: No, I have the brown kind.

'*I'm so thirsty my tongue is hanging out.*'
'Is that what it is? I thought it was your tie.'

CUSTOMER: *Have you smoked salmon, waiter?*
WAITER: No, I've only smoked cigarettes.

What sort of tiles can't be stuck on walls?
Reptiles.

PAUL: *Did you know that the most intelligent person in the world is going deaf?*
JAMES: No, really? Who is it?
PAUL: *Pardon?*

What do you get if you cross an owl with a skunk?
A bird that smells, but doesn't give a hoot.

DOCTOR: I know you're sick, have a very high temperature, and you only live around the corner, but, Mother, you know I never make house calls.

'Then I discovered that if I put my electric toaster under the mattress, it was easy to pop out of bed every morning.'

'*Why do you want to be buried at sea?*'
'My wife says she wants to walk on my grave.'

Why will television never take the place of newspapers?
Have you ever tried swatting a fly with a television?

WIFE: *Is it all right to make breakfast in my nightgown?*
HUSBAND: Yes, but it would be less messy in a frying-pan.

Always be kind to your mother about her cooking and she may help you with the dishes.

What would happen if pigs could fly?
Bacon would go up.

FIRST FLEA: *You're not looking too well.*
SECOND FLEA: No, I don't feel up to scratch.

ALFRED: *I come from a broken home.*
ALBERT: Why was that?
ALFRED: *Dad didn't know there was a gas leak when he lit a match.*

Why is Prince Charles like part of the postal service?
Because he is a royal male.

PATIENT: *I wish I could stop talking to myself.*
PSYCHIATRIST: Why is that?
PATIENT: *I'm a door-to-door salesman and I keep selling myself things I don't want.*

What did the Arab say when he left his friends?
'Oil see you again.'

'*I've just been stung by one of your bees.*'
'Show me which one and I'll punish it.'

UNCLE: *How do you find the dinners at your new school?*
BRIAN: Very hard to take in.

Did you hear the tale about the umbrella?
It was a put-up job.

What did the mouse say when it broke two of its front teeth?
'Hard cheese.'

Where do spiders play football?
Webley.

NEWSFLASH: A baby has been christened 'Glug-glug'.
The vicar fell in the font.

Stupid Stan went to buy a wig. He asked for one that had a hole in the top.

'But if it has a hole in the top people will see that you are bald,' said the wig-maker.

'Yes, I know,' said Stan. 'If people see I'm bald they won't think that I'm wearing a wig.'

Knock, knock.
Who's there?
Warner.
Warner who?
Warner lift? My car's outside.

'*Waiter, there's a dead fly in my soup.*'
'He was so young to die.' (Sob, sob.)

What is a philatelist?
A person of the right stamp.

POLICEMAN: *Madam, your dog has been chasing the postman on his bicycle.*
MRS TUPPER: Don't be silly, officer, my dog can't ride a bicycle.

What is a cow's favourite TV programme?
Dr Moo.

CUSTOMER: *I'll have a drink for starters.*
WAITER: Aperitif, sir?
CUSTOMER: *Yes, I'll have a set of those to eat the steak with afterwards.*

What is a tailor's dummy?
It's what a tailor's baby sucks.

PATIENT: *Doctor, I've got a very sore tongue.*
DOCTOR: Please go to the window and stick your tongue out.
PATIENT: *Will that help?*
DOCTOR: Not at all, it's just that I don't like the neighbours.

Why is there a Mother's Day, a Father's Day, but no Son Day?
Because there is a Sunday in every week.

Knock, knock.
Who's there?
Sonya.
Sonya who?
Sonya foot, I can smell it from here.

A bird in the hand makes it difficult to blow your nose.

A gentleman dining at Crewe,
Found a rather large mouse in his stew.
Said the waiter, 'Don't shout,
Or wave it about,
Or the rest will be wanting one too!'

'*I say, Madam, are all those children yours, or is it a picnic?*'
'They're all mine, and believe me, it's no picnic!'

A little boy at the seaside saw a great big new Rolls-Royce parked on the promenade, and with his metal-ended spade he scratched several deep lines all along the side of it. His father, who was following him, was very angry and hit the boy around the head.
    'What did I tell you?' he shouted. 'If you break that spade, you won't get another one!'

THIEF: *Quick, the police are coming! Jump out of the window!*
ACCOMPLICE: But we're on the thirteenth floor!
THIEF: *This is no time to be superstitious.*

Did you hear about the comedian who was so bad that when he gave a concert in an open-air park twenty-three trees got up and walked away?

Knock, knock.
Who's there?
Ammonia.
Ammonia who?
Ammonia little girl and I can't reach the door.

67

What did the hamburger say to the tomato?
'That's enough of your sauce!'

'I throw myself into every task I undertake.'
'Go and dig a big hole.'

'My grandmother is incredible. She's 102 and hasn't a grey hair in her head. She's completely bald.'

ZIPPY: *I've just bought a pig.*
DIPPY: Where are going to keep it?
ZIPPY: *Under the bed.*
DIPPY: But what about the smell?
ZIPPY: *Oh, he'll soon get used to that.*

'Did you ever see a salad bowl?'
'No, but I did see a horse box.'

What did the leaning tower of Pisa say to Big Ben?
'If you've got the time, I've got the inclination.'

FIRST WOMAN: *I'm going to call my baby Orson, after Orson Welles.*
SECOND WOMAN: What's your surname?
FIRST WOMAN: *Cart.*

TEACHER: *You can't sleep in my class!*
EDWARD: If you didn't speak quite so loud I could.

This year's tug-of-war match between England and France will have to be cancelled unless someone can find a 40-kilometre rope.

What is the difference between teachers and polos?
People like polos.

68

What do angry rodents send to each other at
   Yuletide?
Cross-mouse cards.

Little Miss Muffet
Sat on her tuffet
Eating a bowl of stew.
Along came a spider
And sat down beside her
So she ate him up too.

Why is it dangerous to read a first-aid book?
Because you'll meet with a chapter of accidents.

MOTHER: *When that nasty little boy threw stones at you
   you should have come straight to me, instead of
   throwing stones back at him.*
BOY: Why? You can't throw straight!

'*I understand you buried your husband last week.*'
'I had to – he was dead.'

'*Waiter, is the food good here?*'
'I don't know, I never eat here.'

A man went into a pub with his friend and said: 'I'll have a beer for Donkey, and one for myself.'

The barman turned to the friend and asked: 'Why does he call you Donkey?'

The man replied: 'Eeyore, eeyore, eeyore 'e always calls me that.'

What did Big Chief Running Water call his baby?
Little Drip.

Why do elephants wear sandals?
To stop themselves sinking in the sand.

Why do ostriches bury their heads in the sand?
To look for elephants who have not been wearing sandals.

EDNA: *I'll never know how our house keeps standing, it's such a shack.*
ENID: The woodworm must be holding hands.

FREDA: *Why is the waiter crying?*
FRED: He just burnt his thumb in our soup.

GUEST: *What are your weekly rates?*
HOTEL MANAGER: I don't know. Nobody's ever stayed that long.

'*I want to buy a dress to put on around the house.*'
'Certainly, Madam, how big is your house?'

What do geese watch on TV?
Duckumentaries.

DOCTOR: *How are those pills I prescribed to improve your memory working?*
PATIENT: Which pills?

'My wife must be really ashamed of me.'
'Why do you say that?'
'Last Christmas she knitted me a polo-necked sweater with no hole.'

SIGN NEAR GALLOWS: Don't hang around.

VERA: *Did the music teacher say your voice was heavenly?*
VALDA: Almost. She said it was like nothing on earth.

GIRL: *Did you know that girls are smarter than boys?*
BOY: Really? I never knew that.
GIRL: *There! See what I mean?*

ETHEL: *Tell me more gossip about Carol and Bradley.*
GLADYS: I can't, I've already told you more than I heard myself.

'What kind of work do you do?'
'My boss says it's sloppy.'

What do you get if you dial 69854321660998664238490591415600?
A blister on your finger.

PRINCESS TO KNIGHT: Don't just stand there, slay something.

71

DOCTOR: *Mr Briggs, you must stop thinking that you are a fly.*

MR BRIGGS: How can I do that, Doctor?

DOCTOR: *Well, the first thing you can do is stop walking on the ceiling.*

WIFE: *I'm sorry, darling, but the dog has just eaten your dinner.*

HUSBAND: Don't worry, my sweet, we'll go to the pet shop tomorrow and buy a new dog.

Where do cows go when they want a night out?
To the mooooovies.

'My sister is so modest, she was born wearing a nappy.'

BURGLAR: *The police put me in jail for doing my Christmas shopping early.*
LAWYER: How could they do that?
BURGLAR: *They caught me in the shop at 3 o'clock in the morning.*

PSYCHIATRIST: *Congratulations, Mr Snorkle, you are finally cured of your madness. But why are you sad?*
PATIENT: Wouldn't you be sad if yesterday you were Napoleon and the next day you were nobody?

WIFE: *Shall I offer this tramp one of our cakes?*
HUSBAND: Why, what harm has he ever done us?

'*Did you hear about the scientist who invented a fly paper but couldn't discover the right formula?*'
'Did he give up?'
'*No, he stuck to it.*'

A woman walked into a beauty salon and said to the hairdresser, 'I want to look beautiful. How can I do that?'
The hairdresser looked carefully at the woman and replied:
'Visit the plastic surgeon over the road.'

Did you hear about the loony fisherman?
He baited his book with rubber mice because he wanted to catch catfish.

FRANKIE: *Will you marry me, darling?*
FRANCES: I'm not sure. You've been married seven times already and I've heard some nasty stories about you.
FRANKIE: *Don't believe any of them. They are just old wives' tales.*

'Doctor, what is the most difficult part of an operation?'
'Sewing up the patient. I can't see to thread the needle.'

CROSSWORD FAN: *I've been trying to think of a word for two weeks.*
FRIEND: How about a fortnight?

MAN IN DOCTOR'S WAITING ROOM: I do hope that the ringing in my ears isn't disturbing anyone?

'In Spain the most popular pastime is bullfighting.'
'Bullfighting? Isn't that revolting?'
'No, revolting used to be their favourite pastime. Now it's bullfighting.'

MAN: *Judge, I want a divorce. My wife keeps a pig in our bedroom and the smell is awful.*
JUDGE: Couldn't you open the windows?
MAN: *What! And let all my pigeons out?*

DOCTOR: *How did you come to burn both your ears, Mrs Boswell?*
MRS BOSWELL: Well, I was ironing and the telephone rang. I answered the iron by mistake.
DOCTOR: *So how did you burn the other ear?*
MRS BOSWELL: I'd no sooner hung up when the same person rang again.

'It's tough going through an identity crisis when you're apathetic. You don't know who you are and you couldn't care less about finding out.'

'They tell me that the newspaper is going up tomorrow, so I've been out and bought all the copies I can today.'

FRANKENSTEIN: *Tell me, Igor, where is the Monster?*
IGOR: He's just gone to post twenty Father's Day cards.

What do you call a midget novelist?
A short story writer.

ELSIE: *I'll have you know I can marry anyone I please!*
EDNA: That may be, but you don't please anyone.

MRS P.: *Your husband seems to be a man of rare gifts.*
MRS Q.: He certainly is. It's five years since he gave me anything.

'*Would you wear crocodile shoes?*'
'No, I never wear secondhand clothes.'

MR H.: *Did they get X-rays of your wife's jaw while she was in hospital?*
MR K.: No, they tried, but all they could get were motion pictures.

Don't be disappointed if your dreams never come true. Remember, your nightmares don't either.

What do you get if you cross a man with a goat?
Someone who is always butting into other people's affairs.

75

HERBERT: *Did you hear about the idiot who goes around saying 'No'?*

HORACE: No.

HERBERT: *Oh, it's you, is it?*

MOTORIST: *When I bought this car you said it was rust-free, and look at it! There's rust all over the bottom.*

GARAGE-OWNER: Yes, I sold you the car, but the rust was free.

WIFE: *I can't think where all the grocery money goes!*

HUSBAND: Stand sideways and look in the mirror, then you'll see.

'Did you wash the fish before cooking it?'
'Why wash a fish when it's been in water all its life?'

What happened to the snake with a cold?
She adder viper nose.

Did you hear about the mad professor who invented a waterproof teabag?

PAM: *Are you going to buy a fall-out shelter in case of a nuclear bomb?*

SAM: No, I'll go out afterwards and buy a used one.

Why did the man jump from the top of the Empire State Building?
He wanted to make a hit on Broadway.

What man never worked a whole day in his life?
A night-watchman.

DICK: *My wife wanted to see the world.*
MICK: What did you do?
DICK: *I bought her an atlas.*

'*I once ate a watch.*'
'Wasn't that time-consuming?'

Did you hear about the man who bought a waterproof, shockproof, anti-magnetic, unbreakable watch?
He lost it.

LILY: *If Shakespeare were alive today he would still be a remarkable man.*
TILLY: Yes, he would. He'd be 400 years old.

SHOPKEEPER: *Last week I sold twenty Victorian dresses.*
CUSTOMER: It must have been early clothing day.

'*Waiter, is this pie chicken or beef?*'
'Whatever you ordered, sir.'

'*They say: "Let your smile be your umbrella".*'
'I tried that and got a mouth full of water.'

MAN: *How do you pronounce this country's name – is it 'Hawaii' or 'Havaii'?*
NATIVE: It's pronounced 'Hawaii'.
MAN: *Oh, thank you so much.*
NATIVE: You're velcome.

Did you hear about the twenty-stone woman who got engaged to a twenty-five stone man?
They plan to have a big wedding.

77

WILLIE: *I guess I'll have to go now. Don't trouble to see me to the door.*
AUNTIE MARY: It's no trouble. It will be a pleasure.

FATTY: *They say that travel broadens one.*
SKINNY: My goodness, you must have been around the world.

Why did the man push his bicycle to work?
He was so late that he didn't have time to get on.

'*How far is it to the next town?*'
'Oh, about five miles. You can walk it easily in an hour, if you run.'

Why did the orange break down?
It ran out of juice.

REMEMBER: Your tongue is in a wet place. Don't let it slip.

Knock, knock.
Who's there?
Freddie.
Freddie who?
Freddie or not, here I come!

'*How are the acoustics in this theatre?*'
'They're so good that the actors can hear every cough.'

'*What do you give the man who has everything?*'
'My telephone number.'

With what instrument can you draw teeth painlessly?
A pencil.

78

'*I haven't seen you for weeks, what have you been doing?*'
'Oh, I've been busy. I had a tooth out and a new gas stove put in.'

FRED: *Why do you have carrots sticking out of your ears?*
TED: You'll have to talk louder. I have carrots sticking out of my ears.

Why did the woman keep her blonde wig on the lamp?
Because it was a light shade.

'*Can you swim?*'
'Only in water.'

In Great Britain where are kings and queens usually crowned?
On the head.

What is a metronome?
A dwarf in a British Leyland car.

What did the angry octopus say to the octopus that made him cross?
One of these days –
pow
pow
pow
pow
pow
pow
pow
pow
right in the mouth!

SUSAN: *I just love sunbathing, don't you?*
SARAH: Oh yes, I could sit in the sun all day and all
night.

How do you swim a hundred metres in two seconds?
Swim over a waterfall.

What do you get when you cross rabbits with leeks?
Bunions.

MICHAEL: *I'm going to get up at dawn tomorrow to see
the sun rise.*
CHRISTOPHER: If you'd picked a better time I would have
come with you.

What do they call a by-pass in Wales?
A Dai-version.

MAN IN RESTAURANT: *Will you join me in a bowl of soup?*
WOMAN: Do you think there's room for both of us?

Why did the man wear a lot of clothes to paint his house?
Because it said on the tin: PUT ON THREE COATS.

Why do giraffes have such long necks?
Because their feet smell terrible.

An old lady bought six packets of mothballs and came back to the shop the very next day to buy six more. The assistant looked very surprised.
  'You must have a lot of moths,' he said.
  'Yes,' replied the old lady. 'I spent the whole day throwing these things at them, but I've only hit one so far.'

What do you call a man who shaves twenty times a day?
A barber.

Sign outside a dairy: YOU CAN'T BEAT OUR MILK, BUT YOU CAN WHIP OUR CREAM.

Why did the man ask for alphabet soup?
So that he could read while he was eating.

DOROTHY: *How is your insomnia?*
GWENDOLINE: Worse. I can't even sleep when it's time to get up.

Who wrote an underwater version of Pygmalion?
Jaws Bernard Shaw.

PETER: *I can sing the 'Star Spangled Banner' for hours.*

JONATHAN: So what? I can sing 'Stars and Stripes Forever'.

BEATRICE: *I once sang for the King of Siam.*

CHRISTOBEL: How do you know?

BEATRICE: *Because he said 'Honey, if you're a singer, I'm the King of Siam'.*

'*Can you sing top C?*'
'No, I sing low-sy!'

What is green, has two legs, and a trunk?
A seasick tourist.

Why is a mousetrap like the measles?
Because it's catching.

DANIEL: *I went to see a play last night.*

MONICA: Did it have a happy ending?

DANIEL: *Yes, I was glad when it was over.*

HOW TO CURE A HEADACHE: Thrust your head through a window and the pane will disappear.

FATHER: *Were the shops crowded today?*

MOTHER: So crowded that two women were trying on the same dress.

ACTOR: *I shall never forget my first lines in the theatre.*

FAN: Oh, what were they?

ACTOR: *Peanuts! Choc-ices! Popcorn!*

82

HOW TO PREVENT A HEAD COLD FROM GOING TO YOUR CHEST: Tie a knot in your neck.

Knock, knock.
Who's there?
Dummy.
Dummy who?
Dummy a favour and get lost.

MOTHER: *Why don't you scrape some mud off your shoes?*
HAROLD: What shoes?

TEACHER: *How do you spell 'inconsequentially'?*
PUPIL: Always wrong.

MRS ROBBINS: *I hear you missed school yesterday.*
MARGARET: Not one bit.

Did you know that the wristwatch was invented by a Scotsman because he hated taking anything out of his pockets?

What would the cannibal be who ate his mother's sister?
An aunt-eater.

HUSBAND: *My goodness, what dreadful weather it was last night.*
WIFE: Why didn't you wake me up? You know I can't sleep during a storm.

TICKET COLLECTOR: *I'm sorry, Madam, but your ticket is for Bristol and this train is going to Edinburgh.*
OLD LADY: Well, didn't you ought to tell the driver he's going the wrong way?

PASSENGER: *Does this train stop at Kings Cross station?*
GUARD: Well if it doesn't there'll be one almighty crash.

AGENT: *Is the actress good looking?*
ACTOR: Well, I wouldn't say she's ugly, but she's got a perfect face for radio.

Do you know the story about the body-snatchers?
Well, I won't tell you. You might get carried away.

'Mummy, Mummy, Dad's going out.'
'Well, pour some more paraffin on him, dear.'

TEACHER: *Can you spell a word with more than a hundred letters in it?*
TIMMY: P-O-S-T-O-F-F-I-C-E.

FIRST CANNIBAL: *Am I late for supper?*
SECOND CANNIBAL: Yes, everybody's been eaten.

Why did the Red Indian have a bucket on his head?
Because he was a pale-face.

'*Mummy, Mummy, all the boys at school called me a
    girl!*'
'What did you do?'
'*I hit them with my handbag.*'

POSTMAN: *Oh, Madam, you've put too many stamps on
    this letter.*
LADY CRABTREE: Oh dear, I hope it won't go too far now.

'*Waiter, you have your thumb on my steak!*'
'Well, I don't want it to fall on the floor again.'

GARY: *I am so unpopular in school, everybody hates me.*
LARRY: Well, I'm so unpopular my phone doesn't ring even when I'm in the bath.

CHEMIST: *Certainly, Sir, we make life-size enlargements of photographs.*
MAN: Good, here's a picture of an elephant.

WOMAN: *I don't like this photo, it doesn't do me justice.*
MAN: It's mercy you want, not justice.

SAMMY: *I used to be twins.*
SALLY: How do you know?
SAMMY: *My mother has a picture of me when I was two.*

Did you hear about the parents who were so proud of their baby son that they used to have him kidnapped just to see his picture in the papers?

GEORGE: *I'm not feeling myself tonight.*
WINIFRED: I thought I noticed an improvement.

STEPHEN: *Did you go to Nigel's party?*
FIONA: No, the invitation said 'from four to nine' and I'm ten.

What is bacon's favourite song?
'Fry Me to the Moon'.

Why are dumplings unfortunate?
They're always getting into a stew.

What do you get if you cross a whale with a duckling?
Moby Duck.

86

BERYL: *Clem is a most wonderful person.*
MERYL: Is that your honest opinion?
BERYL: *No, it's his.*

What is chocolate outside, peanut inside, and sings hymns?
A Sunday School Treat.

What is the best feature of Italy?
Only a Roman knows! (nose)

What did Juliet say when she met Romeo on the balcony?
'Couldn't you get seats in the stalls?'

DANNY: *My rich uncle owns a newspaper.*
BENNY: So what? A newspaper only costs 20p.

REMEMBER: A hole may be nothing at all, but you can break your neck in it.

MAN IN STREET: *Can you tell me how you get to the London Palladium?*
OLD LADY: It takes a lot of talent, sir. What can you do?

Two racehorses met in a paddock. One said to the other, 'Your pace is familiar, but I'm afraid I don't remember your mane.'

Did you hear about the tennis player who was taken to court for making a racket?

VERA: *Can you play the piano?*
IRMA: I don't know – I've never tried.

HEADMASTER: *Do you think teenagers should wear lipstick?*
TEACHER: Only girl teenagers.

What is never seen but often changed.
Your mind.

FLORA: *I've changed my mind.*
DORA: Does it work any better?

HARRY HANDFULL: *Officer, I've just found this wig in the street.*
PC PUDDLEDOCK: Then take it to a psychiatrist.
HARRY HANDFULL: *Why should I take it to a psychiatrist?*
PC PUDDLEDOCK: Well, it's obviously off its head.

Wishing to please his wife, a man went into a florist's shop to buy her some anemones, her favourite flowers. But the shopkeeper only had bunches of decorative green fern, so the man presented these to his wife apologetically.

'Never mind, darling,' she smiled, 'with fronds like these who needs anemones?'

Bad luck is bending down to pick up a four-leaf clover and being attacked by poison ivy.

JIMMY: *I'm so unlucky, my artificial flower died.*
TIMMY: Not as unlucky as me, aspirins give me a headache.
JIMMY: *That's nothing. I went to the swimming pool and it caught fire!*

LOST – a black poodle by old lady who answers to the name of Sooty.

Eric the Red was a Norse of a different colour.

BOB: *How long can a man live without a brain?*
TOM: I don't know. How old are you?

SARAH: *My little brother has just fallen down a manhole.*
What shall I do?
SIMON: Dash to the library and get a book on how to raise
a child.

MOTHER: *Melanie, your stockings are all wrinkled.*
MELANIE: Mother, I'm not wearing any stockings. . . .

'They laughed when I invented a new kind of dynamite,
but when I dropped it they exploded.'

MAUREEN: *I speak eight languages.*
DOREEN: It's a pity you speak them all at the same
time.

TED: *I passed your house yesterday.*
FRED: Thanks, I appreciate it.

Did you hear about the man who always wore
sunglasses?
He took a dim view of things.

ELECTRICIAN: *I've come to repair your doorbell, Madam.*
LADY CONSTANCE: You should have come yesterday.
ELECTRICIAN: *I did! I rang the bell five times and got no*
answer.

Do you know what you look like when you are asleep?
Well, just look at yourself in the mirror with your
eyes closed.

What do you do when you see a big fierce lion?
Hope that he doesn't see you.

Knock, knock.
Who's there?
Wooden Shoe.
Wooden Shoe who?
Wooden Shoe like to know!

MAN: *How do I get to the general hospital?*
POLICEMAN: Stand in the middle of the road for a few
    seconds.

How do you make a slow racehorse fast?
Don't feed him.

Why did the jockey name his horse 'Radish'?
So that he could say: 'Here's my horseradish.'

SIGN OUTSIDE A BUTCHER'S SHOP: Pleased to meet you:
meat to please you.

Why did the little girl stand on her head?
She was turning things over in her mind.

THOMAS: *Your hat is on the wrong way.*
RENÉE: How do you know which way I'm going?

HARRY: *What happened to that dopey blonde Roger used
    to go around with?*
PAMELA: I dyed my hair.

When is a car not a car?
When it turns into a garage.

90

'I bought a barometer in Japan.'
'Who wants to know if it's raining in Yokohama?'

Sign outside a hairdressers: WE CURL UP AND DYE
FOR YOU.

WINNIE: *Why did you send me an empty box for my birthday?*
GEOFF: Well, at least when I send you nothing I like to wrap it up nicely.

What did the rake say to the hoe?
Hi, hoe!

MRS BROWN: *Don't you have any friends to play with?*
VERONICA: Oh yes, I have friends, but I hate them.

How did Little Bo-Peep lose her sheep?
She had a crook with her.

What is the best way to catch a fish?
Get someone to throw it at you.

'I entered a face-making contest.'
'You did! And who won second prize?'

Why did the chicken walk over the hill?
Because it couldn't walk under it.

MILLICENT: *My grandfather lived to be ninety-five and never used glasses.*
PRUDENCE: Well, lots of people drink straight from the bottle.

What knocks you senseless every night but doesn't hurt you?
Sleep.

Why do Eskimos eat whale meat and blubber?
You'd blubber too if you had to eat whale meat.

DANNY: *I can lift an elephant with one hand.*
FANNY: I've never seen a one-handed elephant.

MOTHER: *I never told lies when I was a child.*
LITTLE MICKEY: Oh, when did you begin?

SISSIE: *I hear your brother is a conductor. Musical or on the buses?*
SILLIE: Electrical. He was struck by lightning.

What's round and purple and bad at cooking?
Alfred the Grape.

What is a cheerful pachyderm?
A happy-potamus.

What is bright yellow, weighs a ton, has four legs and sings?
Two half-ton canaries.

Which cartoon character loves sausages?
Meaty Mouse.

Knock, knock.
Who's there?
Canoe.
Canoe who?
Canoe come out and play with me?

LENNY: *I washed my parrot in Cleanshine and it died.*

BENNY: *I told you not to wash it in Cleanshine.*

LENNY: *Oh, it wasn't the Cleanshine that killed it, it was the spin-dryer.*

What is extremely tall and goes 'Eef if of muf'?
A backward giant.

GORDON: *We're having Aunt Minnie for Christmas dinner this year.*

BARBARA: Well, she can't possibly be tougher than last year's turkey!

MAN: *I went home last night to find my son in our lounge sitting in front of a blazing fire.*

FRIEND: Well, what's wrong with that?

MAN: *We haven't got a fireplace.*

'*My father was a Pole.*'
'Oh, North or South?'

MARY: *I hear egg shampoo is good for your hair.*
ANNIE: Yes, but how do you get a chicken to lay an egg on your head?

BERYL: *I play the piano by ear.*
BRIAN: Doesn't it interfere with your earrings?

What smells most in any garden?
Your nose.

MAN: *Help! I've just given my wife her prescription and find you've given me arsenic instead of a sleeping powder.*
CHEMIST: That's OK. You only owe me another 50p.

DORRIE: *I know a dog worth £50000.*
FLORRIE: My goodness, how could a dog save so much?

WIFE: *I want you to keep that dog out of the house, it's full of fleas.*
HUSBAND: Fido, don't go in the house, it's full of fleas.

Doctor, Doctor, every bone in my body hurts.
Well, just be thankful you're not a herring.

Did you hear about the man who discovered a cure for amnesia, but kept forgetting what it was?

DENTIST: *Now behave yourself. I haven't touched your tooth yet.*
BOBBY: I know, but you're standing on my foot.

DENTIST: *Now be a good boy and say 'Ah' so that I can get my finger out of your mouth.*

How can you hammer in nails without hitting your thumb?
Get somebody else to hold the nail.

MR BROWN: *I didn't know that your wife was so good at dancing the Charleston.*
MR JONES: She isn't. The waiter just spilled some hot soup down her back.

Where do musicians often live?
In A flat.

PASSENGER: *Conductor, do you stop at the Savoy Hotel?*
CONDUCTOR: What, on my salary? Certainly not.

Knock, knock.
Who's there?
Minerva.
Minerva who?
Minerva-s wreck from all these questions.

Which is faster – heat or cold?
Heat, because you can catch cold.

What's musical and handy in a supermarket?
A Chopin Liszt.

TEACHER: *Name five things that contain milk.*
KENNETH: That's easy. Ice cream, butter, cheese and
   two cows.

What do owls sing when it is raining hard?
'Too-wet-to-woo.'

HOSPITAL VISITOR: *Does your wife miss you a lot?*
BANDAGED PATIENT: No, she's a very good shot. That's
   why I'm in here.

DINER: *Waiter, this milk is weak.*
WAITER: Well, the cow got caught in the rain.

JUDGE: *Guilty. Ten days in prison or £100 fine.*
PRISONER: I'll take the £100.

Did you hear about the cannibal that only ate beans?
Human beans.

DR DOOB: *I spent three years in college taking
   Medicine.*
MISS THICK: Oh, and are you feeling any better now?

Knock, knock.
Who's there?
Dishes.
Dishes who?
Dishes me. Who ish you?

'*How long do you cook spaghetti?*'
'Oh, about twenty centimetres.'

Why does an elephant have a trunk?
So that he has somewhere to hide if he sees a mouse.

Did you hear about the cow who was so cold in winter
that she gave nothing but ice cream?

MRS WHITE: *How do you like my biscuits?*
MRS BLACK: Very good. Did you buy them yourself?

'*Do you feel like a cup of coffee?*'
'Of course not, do I look like one?'

Why did the parents call their baby 'Coffee'?
Because he kept them awake all night.

Thought for the day: in England we drink our coffee out of cups. In China they drink their tea out of doors.

MRS STARCH: *That dress fits you like a bandage.*
MRS SPICE: Yes, I bought it by accident.

DORIS: *How come you're wearing only one glove? Did you lose one?*
MAURICE: No, I found one!

BILLY: *What's the weather like?*
SILLY: I don't know, it's so foggy I can't see.

'*Mummy, we're pretending to be elephants at the zoo, will you help us?*'
'Of course, dear. What am I to do?'
'*Well, you're the lady that feeds us with buns.*'

BOSS: *Why were you late for work?*
JOSH: Well there are eight of us in our family and the alarm was set for seven.

Why did the lady mop up her spilt tea with a piece of cake?
It was a sponge cake.

MOTHER: *Why did you put a mouse in your sister's bed?*
TIMMY: Because I couldn't find a frog.

What does a Hindu?
It lays eggs.

'Why is your little sister crying?'
''Cos she just came down the stairs without walking.'

POLICEMAN: *Did you not see the 30 mph sign?*
MOTORIST: No, Officer, I was driving to fast to see it.

WIFE: *I'm not sure I like this 'bananas-only' diet that the doctor has put me on. It seems to be having a very strange effect.*
HUSBAND: Don't be silly, dear. Now if you'll just stop scratching yourself and come down from the curtains. . . .

What should a prize fighter drink?
Punch.

TEACHER: *Now, Phyllis, your brother gave me exactly the same essay as yours about a picnic.*
PHYLLIS: Well, Miss, it was the same picnic.

'Have you read Dickens?'
'No, but I have red pyjamas.'

WIFE ON SHIP: *I've put all our clothes in that little cupboard with the glass window.*
HUSBAND: You idiot! That's the porthole.

'I've just come back from the beauty parlour.'
'Shame it was closed.'

MRS BEAN: *My husband says I'm the most beautiful woman in the world.*
MRS GONE: Yes, my husband's got poor eyesight too.

JOHN: *Do you always bathe in muddy water?*
TOM: It wasn't muddy when I got in.

BARBER: *You say you've been here before? I don't remember your face.*
CUSTOMER: Oh, it's all healed up now.

What goes 'Ho, ho, ho, plop'?
Santa Claus laughing his head off.

Why did the little girl put a calendar in her piggy bank?
Because she wanted to save time.

Knock, knock.
Who's there?
Bella.
Bella who?
Bella no ringa, thatsa why I knock, knock.

CUSTOMER: *Are you the man that cut my hair last time?*
BARBER: No, sir, I've only been working here for two years.

What is the perfect cure for dandruff?
Baldness.

Did you hear about the absent-minded baby-sitter who put the TV to bed and sat and watched the baby?

What did the dog say when he sat on some sandpaper?
Ruff.

BILLY: *Dad, what's nuclear fission?*
FATHER: Er . . . I'm afraid I don't know anything about atomic energy.
BILLY: *Well, how does a space ship land on the moon if there's no gravity there?*
FATHER: Well, I don't really know about space travel either.
BILLY: *Oh. Can you tell me how jets assist a take-off then?*
FATHER: That's a bit too complicated to explain.
BILLY: *You don't mind me asking you all these questions, do you, Dad?*
FATHER: Of course not, Son. You have to ask questions if you want to learn anything.

'*Can you telephone from a plane?*'
'Of course I can tell a phone from a plane, the plane's got wings.'

WIFE: *But, Henry, that isn't our baby!*
HUSBAND: I know, but it's a much better pram.

'*Excuse me, Stewardess, but why is the pilot laughing hysterically?*'
'He's thinking of what they will say at the asylum when they discover he has escaped.'

Sign in golf club: BACK SOON. GONE TO TEE.

'*I'm a well-known collector of antiques.*'
'I know, I've seen your wife.'

102

JAVEY: (*answering telephone*) Hello.
VOICE: Hello. Is Boo there?
JAVEY: *Boo who?*
VOICE: Don't cry, little boy. I must have got the wrong number.

Want to upset someone? Dash into an antique shop and ask 'What's new?'

Knock, knock.
Who's there?
Yvonne.
Yvonne who?
Yvonne to be alone.

LITTLE GIRL: I was going to buy you some hankies for your birthday, Grandad, but I couldn't remember the size of your nose.

'*How did you have this accident?*'
'Well, the sign said STOP-LOOK-LISTEN! – and while I did a train hit me.'

The best way to remember something is to try and forget it!

DOCTOR: *You are now completely cured of gambling.*
PATIENT: Good – and I bet you £10 I won't let it happen again.

FIRST CANNIBAL: *How did the missionary go down?*
SECOND CANNIBAL: Oh very well. We've ordered another one for next Christmas.

TEACHER: *Suppose a mother had eight children, but only six potatoes. How could she give them all a fair share?*
ROBIN: Give them mashed potato, Miss.

How do you make jumping beans?
Get some beans, go up behind them and shout 'Boo!'

MOLLIE: *I was so embarrassed when they asked me to take off my mask at the Hallowe'en party.*
DOLLIE: Why?
MOLLIE: *Because I wasn't wearing one.*

Mr Boswell saw a small group of boys grouped around a little puppy.

'What are you doing?' he asked.

'Well,' said one boy, 'we're swapping lies and the one who tells the biggest lie gets the puppy.'

'Why!' exclaimed Mr Boswell, 'when I was your age I never thought of telling lies.'

'OK, Mr Boswell,' said the boy, 'the dog's yours. You win.'

'Doctor, this is the third operating table you've ruined this week. You must learn not to cut so deeply.'

Knock, knock.
Who's there?
Hair.
Hair who?
Hair today and gone tomorrow.

What has to be taken before you get it?
A photograph.

104

GEORGE: *I only weighed one kilogram when I was born.*
GORDON: That's not much, did you live?
GEORGE: *Did I live! You should see me now.*

'*Have you ever seen a horse that could count?*'
'No, but I've seen a spelling bee.'

What do misers do in cold weather?
Sit around a candle.

What do misers do in very cold weather?
Light it.

'*Do you think it will rain?*'
'It all depends on the weather.'

TEACHER: *Iceland is as big as Siam. Now then, Jimmy, are you paying attention? How big is Iceland?*
JIMMY: As big as you are, Sir.

What did the bull say when he swallowed a bomb?
'Abominable!'

Five tomatoes – which one was the cowboy?
None, they were all redskins.

PATIENT: *What's the best thing for flat feet?*
DOCTOR: Have you tried a footpump?

'My husband is so lazy. To see if it's raining he calls the dog in to find out if he's wet.'

WITCH IN HOSPITAL: *I'm feeling a lot better.*
DOCTOR: You can get up for a spell this afternoon.

'*But I don't want to go to Australia, Mummy.*'
'Shut up and keep swimming.'

SIMON: *When I grow up I'm going to drive a steam roller.*
FATHER: Well I won't stand in your way.

Knock, knock.
Who's there?
Luke.
Luke who?
Luke who's talking.

LANDLADY: *Do you have a good memory for faces?*
TENANT: Yes, why?
LANDLADY: *There's no mirror in the bathroom.*

HUSBAND TO MOTHER-IN-LAW: Look pleasant. As soon as I've taken the photograph you can assume your normal expression.

MR SMITH: *I just met a man whom I haven't seen for twenty years.*
MR JONES: That's nothing, I just met a man whom I never saw before in my life.

MRS JOHNSON: My son Eric is so polite. He always takes his shoes off before putting his feet on the table.

DOCTOR: *Good morning, Mrs Butler. I haven't seen you for a long time.*
MRS BUTLER: I know, Doctor, I've been ill.

If a white chicken fell into a purple puddle what would he be?
Wet.

Little Avril decided to take parachute lessons. When she was ready to make her first jump, all her friends and relations gathered on the ground to watch her. Avril jumped from the plane and laughed and laughed to herself all the way down. She knew that she was going to fool them all because she wasn't wearing a parachute.

BARBARA: *Was the weather hot on your holiday?*
PEARL: Hot! It was so hot we couldn't stand it in the shade, we had to go out in the sun.

'*I didn't come here to be insulted!*'
'Oh, where do you usually go?'

What did the baby mouse say when he saw a bat for the first time?
'Mummy, I've just seen an angel.'

A young man gave his girlfriend a sparkling necklace for her birthday.

'Oooh,' she exclaimed, 'are they real diamonds?'

'They'd better be,' he replied, 'or else I've been swindled out of 50p.'

Why did the baby strawberry cry?
His mother was in a jam.

How does a pixie eat?
By goblin.

'I know a dog who eats garlic. His bark is much worse than his bite.'

BORIS: *Doctor, I'm worried about my friend.*
He thinks he's a lift.
DOCTOR: I'd better see him. Send him up to me will you?
BORIS: *I can't. He doesn't stop at your floor.*

More Beaver Books

We hope you have enjoyed this Beaver Book. Her are some of the other titles:

The Beaver Book of Skool Verse A Beaver original. An amazing collection of poems and verses about school, including playground rhymes and games, mnemonics, verses about school dinners, lessons, teachers, end of term and exams. Lots of the material came from children all over the country who sent in their favourite rhymes, and the collection was put together by Jennifer Curry, with cartoons by Graham Thompson

The Kids' Book of Games A large-format book containing an almost endless selection of mind- and finger-boggling activities — things to make, magic tricks, card games, word games, games to play with friends and games to play alone. Written by Rudi McToots and profusely illustrated

William the Wizard When William decides to spend his holidays doing the Community Wizard training course, part 1, he little realises what scrapes he will get into! An amusing story for younger readers by Barbara Cleveland-Peck; illustrated by Sophie Kittredge

These and many other Beavers are available from your local bookshop or newsagent, or can be ordered direct from: Hamlyn Paperback Cash Sales, PO Box 11, Falmouth, Cornwall TR10 9EN. Send a cheque or postal order for the price of the book plus postage at the following rates:
UK: 45p for the first book, 20p for the second book, and 14p for each additional book ordered to a maximum of £1.63;
BFPO and Eire: 45p for the first book, 20p for the second book, plus 14p per copy for the next 7 books and thereafter 8p per book;
OVERSEAS: 75p for the first book and 21p for each extra book.

New Beavers are published every month and if you would like the *Beaver Bulletin,* a newsletter which tells you about new books and gives a complete list of titles and prices, send a large stamped addressed envelope to:

Beaver Bulletin
Arrow Books Limited
17-21 Conway Street
London W1P 6JD

206092